Helping Children Understand the Ministry of Ellen White

Who was Ellen White?

Helping Children Understand the Ministry of Ellen White

Jerry D. Thomas

Pacific Press® Publishing Association

Nampa, Idaho
Oshawa, Ontario, Canada
www.pacificpress.com

Cover design by Gerald Lee Monks
Cover design resources from dreamstime.com / iStockphoto.com
Cover picture of Jesus by Darrel Tank
Inside design by Steve Lanto

Illustration credits:

Harry Anderson—pp. 17, 19, 21, 27
iStockphoto.com—pp. 33, 37, 43, 59, 61
Marcus Mashburn—pp. 15, 23, 25, 29, 31, 35, 39, 41, 45, 47, 49, 51, 53, 55, 63, 65, 67, 69
Sermonview—p. 57
All photos of children on the left-hand pages are from dreamstime.com / iStockphoto.com

Copyright © 2017 by Pacific Press® Publishing Association
Printed in the United States of America
All rights reserved

The author assumes full responsibility for the accuracy
of all facts and quotations as cited in this book.

Additional copies of this book are available by calling toll-free 1-800-765-6955
or by visiting http://www.AdventistBookCenter.com.

Library of Congress Cataloging-in-Publication Data

Names: Thomas, Jerry D., 1959- author.
Title: Who was Ellen White? / Jerry D. Thomas.
Description: Nampa, Idaho : Pacific Press Publishing Association, 2017. |
  Audience: Ages 6-9.
Identifiers: LCCN 2017015628 | ISBN 9780816361823 (pbk. : alk. paper)
Subjects: LCSH: White, Ellen Gould Harmon, 1827-1915—Juvenile literature.
Classification: LCC BX6193.W5 T47 2017 | DDC 286.7092 [B] —dc23 LC record available at https://lccn.loc.gov/2017015628

April 2017

Dedication

For Jennifer,

who at one time confused Ellen White with Helen Keller.

Ouch.

Also by
Jerry D. Thomas

Blessings

The Cat in the Cage and Other Great Stories for Kids

Conversations With Jesus

Messiah

The Midnight Raccoon Alarm and Other Stories

Step by Step

A Thoughtful Hour

A Thoughtful Hour 2

What We Believe for Kids

Detective Zack series

Shoebox Kids series

Contents

Note for Grown-ups.. 11

Introduction: Who Was Ellen White? 13

1. Ellen White Was a Young Girl 14
2. Ellen White Was a Teenager Who Believed Jesus Was Coming Soon ... 16
3. Ellen White Was a Messenger for God 18
4. Ellen White Was a Wife 20
5. Ellen White Was a Writer for God... 22
6. Ellen White Listened to Angels 24
7. Ellen White Saw Visions From God 26
8. Ellen White Wrote Down Visions From God 28
9. Ellen White Believed in Eating Healthy Food 30
10. Ellen White Taught About Health 32
11. Ellen White Was the Mother of Four Boys 34
12. Ellen White Was a Woman Who Loved Mountains and Adventure 36
13. Ellen White Was a Woman Who Went Where God Led Her............. 38
14. Ellen White Was a Woman Who Wanted to Talk About Jesus 40
15. Ellen White Wrote Messages for the Whole World 42

16 Ellen White Loved to Tell the Story of Jesus 44

17 Ellen White Believed in Adventist Education 46

18 Ellen White Wrote Books About God's Love 48

19 Ellen White Gave Offerings for God's Work 50

20 Ellen White Was Guided by Angels 52

21 Ellen White Was Kind to Everyone 54

22 Ellen White Was Protected by Angels 56

23 Ellen White Received Messages for Her Family 58

24 Ellen White Trusted God to Keep His Promises 60

25 Ellen White Loved Her Grandchildren 62

26 Ellen White Liked to Have Fun With Her Family 64

27 Ellen White Loved Family Worship 66

28 Ellen White Was God's Messenger 68

The Williamsport Camp Meeting 72

Brighton Camp Meeting, Victoria, Australia 74

The Health Reform Vision 76

Gift of a Horse and Carriage 78

Note for Grown-ups

I've always had a burden to make difficult things easier to understand. Too often when we talk about God and religion, we throw around words that we don't really understand. It's even worse when we do that while talking with children. We use words they don't know to talk about beliefs they don't understand.

One of the unique challenges in our church is understanding the ministry of Ellen White and how it should impact us as Adventists. This can be especially confusing for children. If we want them to become lifelong Adventists, with faith in the Bible and in our church's doctrines, then we must make sure they are well grounded in what we believe. We must make sure that they learn to appreciate the blessing our church has received from the ministry of our prophet, Ellen White.

In this book, children can learn about the life, ministry, and writings of Ellen White. Stories from her childhood to her retirement years will help them to see her as a real person—a child, a wife, a mother, and a grandmother. They can learn about the important messages God gave her in visions and dreams. Finally, and most important, the book can help children to build faith in God's church and in His prophet.

If you don't feel that you've understood Ellen White's ministry or writings yourself, take this opportunity to study them again for yourself. At the back of the book are recommended books or resources that will give you or the children you care for more stories and more information from that time in Ellen White's life.

I was blessed in writing this book, and I believe you will be blessed as you read it with a child you love.

Jerry D. Thomas

Introduction: Who Was Ellen White?

Way back, a long time ago, when our church first began, one of the most important leaders was Ellen White. She didn't start the Seventh-day Adventist Church by herself, but she was one of the people who helped it begin to grow from a few members, who could fit under one tent, to a church with millions of members around the world.

People at church talk about Ellen White a lot. But do you know who she was? That's what we're going to talk about in this book. Who was Ellen White, and why do we still listen to the things she had to say? I hope this helps you understand more about her and her work for our church.

CHAPTER 1

Ellen White Was a Young Girl

Questions for Grown-ups

1. What do you think about Ellen White?

2. Will learning more about her life help you understand her messages?

For more stories about Ellen's childhood, read *Ellen, the Girl With Two Angels* (see p. 71).

Do you know which day is your birthday? It's the day you were born! Some people were born on May 1. Some were born on July 7. Some were born on October 12. What day were you born on?

On November 26, way back in 1827, two girls were born into the Harmon family on a farm near the town of Gorham, Maine. They were twins! The parents named one girl Ellen and the other one Elizabeth. The girls had a large family. With two brothers and four sisters, they lived in a very busy house! On the farm, they chased cows and dogs and helped in the garden.

After a few years, the family moved to the town of Portland, Maine, where Mr. Harmon worked as a hatmaker. All of the kids helped in the hat-making business whenever they could. Before long, Ellen and Elizabeth went to school. Then one day, when they were nine years old, something terrible happened.

Ellen and Elizabeth were walking home from school. As they walked through a park, an older girl who was angry threw a big rock at them. It hit Ellen right in the face, and she fell to the ground. Elizabeth helped get her home, but Ellen didn't wake up for three weeks.

Without hospitals, such as we have today, Ellen didn't get well for a long time. In fact, she never went to school again. She was too weak to go out and play with other children. For a long time, her face and nose hurt every day. But she did go to church every week with her family. When she was twelve years old, she gave her heart to Jesus. When she was fourteen, she was baptized and became a member of her parents' church.

Who was Ellen White? She was a young girl. She grew up a long time ago. She was hurt and had to stop going to school. And she learned to love Jesus.

Teaching Tips

1. Ask each child: When is your birthday? How old will you be at the next one?

2. We learned about Ellen's injury. Have you ever been hurt badly? What happened?

3. Have you given your heart to Jesus like Ellen did?

Adventist Beliefs for Kids – **15**

CHAPTER 2

Ellen White Was a Teenager Who Believed Jesus Was Coming Soon

Questions for Grown-ups

1. What would you do if you really believed that Jesus was returning in one year?

2. What would you think if someone told you that God was speaking to him or her in vision?

For more information on this topic, see *Accepting Ellen White* (see p. 71).

When she was a teenager, Ellen and her family went to church. They heard a preacher named William Miller. "Jesus is coming soon," Pastor Miller preached. "Look at what the Bible says." Then he talked about prophecies—verses from the Bible that talked about the future. "Jesus will come in just a few years!"

Many more people listened to William Miller. Before long, thousands of people were studying the Bible, and they also believed that Jesus would come very soon. The prophecies seemed to say that Jesus would return in October 1844. Ellen would only be seventeen years old!

Do you ever count down the days until your birthday? Or to Christmas? Ellen and her family starting counting down the days until Jesus would come and take them to heaven. The Harmons began selling the things in their house. They gave all their money to a special newspaper that could be sent out to tell even more people about Jesus and His soon return.

When the special day in October came—October 22—thousands of people woke up early to start watching the sky to see Jesus and His angels coming to take them to heaven. They waited all morning, but Jesus didn't

16 – *Who Was Ellen White?*

come. They waited all afternoon, but Jesus didn't come. They waited all night, but Jesus didn't come. Everyone was very sad and disappointed.

Ellen and her family went home. "What happened?" they asked each other with tears in their eyes. While some people stopped believing, Ellen and her family kept studying the Bible and praying. Not many days later, Ellen met some friends, and together they prayed and studied. While they were praying, God sent Ellen a vision. A vision is like a dream, but you're not asleep.

In her vision, Ellen saw the people who believed in Jesus' return, or advent, as it was also called. She saw them moving along a path to heaven. The ones who kept believing kept moving closer to heaven. The ones who didn't believe fell off the path and were gone. When the vision was over, she told her friends what she had seen. They felt better after they knew that they were still on the path to heaven.

Who was Ellen White? She was a girl who believed that Jesus was coming soon. And she was someone that God talked to through visions.

Teaching Tips

1. What day did you count down to last? Your birthday? Christmas? Summer vacation?

2. Do you think Jesus is coming soon? Why?

3. Ellen and her family were disappointed when Jesus didn't come. Have you ever been disappointed when you were expecting something to happen?

Adventist Beliefs for Kids

CHAPTER 3

Ellen White Was a Messenger for God

Questions for Grown-ups

1. Would you have been able to stand up in front of people and deliver messages like God asked Ellen to do?

2. Is God asking you to do something? Are you ready to move forward, believing that God will give you the strength to do it?

Have you ever been given a message to deliver? Maybe it was a happy message to your brothers or sisters. "Mom says it's time for dinner." Or maybe it was an unhappy message to the other kids in your class. "The teacher says that it's time for recess to be over."

When everyone was sad that Jesus hadn't come back in October 1844, God gave Ellen messages to deliver through her visions. God wanted Ellen to tell people what she had seen. But Ellen was afraid. She didn't like to stand up in front of people and talk. She didn't like to give unhappy messages to people.

What about you? Have you been asked to stand up in front of the church and say a prayer or a memory verse? It's not easy to talk in front of a lot of people, is it? It was hard for Ellen too.

But her friends and family encouraged her to listen to God. "If God has asked you to do this, He will give you the strength to do it," they said. And so Ellen began to travel from one town to another, even though it was winter and the snow made it hard for her horse to pull the carriage. She told believers about her visions and shared the messages God had given her.

Her sister traveled with her, but sometimes it was dangerous for just the two of them to travel from town to town. A young preacher named James White heard Ellen's messages, and he wanted to help. He would often travel with Ellen and her sister, making sure that they arrived safely even if the weather was bad or if bad people threatened to hurt them.

People didn't always listen to Ellen or believe that her messages were from God. But she did what God asked her to do. She shared what she saw in her visions.

Who was Ellen White? She was a messenger. When God showed her something in a vision, she shared that message with everyone who would listen.

Teaching Tips

1. What was the last message you were asked to deliver by a parent or a teacher? Did you deliver it?

2. Have you ever stood up in front of people to say or sing something? (This might be a good time to plan a program where the children can present memory verses or songs at church.)

3. Ellen did what God asked her to do. Do you? What has God asked you to do?

Adventist Beliefs for Kids –

CHAPTER 4

Ellen White Was a Wife

Questions for Grown-ups

1. Do you think it was a good idea for Ellen to marry James? Did that help her work or hinder it?

2. When did you learn about the Sabbath? What convinced you that it is a Bible truth?

Can you imagine what heaven looks like? Do you think about flying like a bird or playing with wild animals? Maybe you would like to soar through space or eat all your favorite foods or see all your favorite people. Do you think about meeting people from the Bible stories? Sometimes when Ellen had visions, she saw heaven and she saw Jesus!

Ellen continued to travel to churches and people's homes and share the things God showed her. In one vision, she saw the new earth that Jesus will create for His followers. She saw a long silver table covered with many different kinds of fruits. "Can I eat some of the fruit?" she asked Jesus.

Jesus told her, "Not now. But in a little while, if you are faithful, you will be able to eat as much fruit as you want. Now you must go back and tell others what I have shown to you."* Ellen carried Jesus' messages just as He asked.

Do you ever want to get married? Maybe a long time from now? Ellen wasn't worried about getting married. She was busy working to tell others about God's love. But she saw James White again before long. She learned that his favorite thing to do was to tell others about Jesus too. They decided to tell others together.

James and Ellen got married in August 1846, and then they could travel together all the time. Before long, they met a sea captain named Joseph Bates who wanted to teach them something new. Captain Bates didn't sail a ship anymore—now he spent all his time preaching and studying the Bible.

"Let me teach you something from the Bible," he said. Then he showed them what the Bible says about God's special seventh-day Sabbath. They studied and decided that Captain Bates was right. From then on, they kept God's Sabbath day every week.

Who was Ellen White? She was a wife. And she learned to keep the seventh-day Sabbath.

---
* Ellen G. White, *Christian Experience and Teachings of Ellen G. White* (Nampa, ID: Pacific Press® Pub. Assn., 1999), 64; author's paraphrase.

Teaching Tips

1. What do you think you'll like most about heaven?

2. What is your favorite kind of fruit? Do you think you'll want to eat it in heaven?

3. Do you ever want to get married like Ellen did? Why would you get married?

Adventist Beliefs for Kids – 21

CHAPTER 5

Ellen White Was a Writer for God

Questions for Grown-ups

1. Do you think you could write as often as Ellen did? Do you feel as though God has given you something to say?

2. Are we willing to work as hard as James and Ellen did to get the message of God's love to the world? Why not?

Do you like to write words on paper? Have you written a story about your family or a report on your vacation? Writing can be hard to do! What if someone told you that you needed to write sixty-four pages of words? You would need to have something very important to say!

Ellen and James continued to travel around, talking with people and teaching them about God's Word. Sometimes they rode the train. Sometimes they were in a carriage or on a sleigh being pulled by a strong horse. But they still wanted to share God's love with more people.

So they started writing their words down. Now they didn't have a computer to type the words into. They had pieces of paper and a pen or pencil. Often James would work all day helping a farmer with his crops or chopping trees into firewood. When he came home at night, he would write words and get the paper ready to take to the printer.

Ellen wrote too. She wrote about the things God had shown her in visions. She wrote about the things she was learning when she studied the Bible. And she also wrote about the places they traveled to and the people they met there.

Every few weeks James took eight pages to a printer. The printer used a machine to make copies. It wasn't like the copiers we have today, but it did the job. When it was ready, James could mail his little newspaper out to people whom they had met or who wanted to learn more.

Ellen kept writing and writing. She wrote while they rode on trains. She wrote at the kitchen table with only a candle for light. She wrote early in the morning and late at night. Finally, she had a whole book—sixty-four pages long—ready to be printed. James took her book to the printer, and soon they had copies to give away to people who wanted to learn more about the Bible and more about God's love.

Who was Ellen White? She was a writer who wanted to tell everyone about God's Word and His love.

Teaching Tips

1. Ask the children to write a story about their families or to tell the story if they aren't able to write.

2. Was it hard for Ellen and James to write so much? Why did they do it?

3. Why did James and Ellen want to print the things they wrote and mail them to others?

Adventist Beliefs for Kids

CHAPTER 6

Ellen White Listened to Angels

Questions for Grown-ups

1. Does it surprise you that an angel would speak to Ellen about something as trivial as a horse?

2. Can you think of a time when God delivered something needed at just the right moment?

For more information on this topic, see "Sketches and Memories of James and Ellen G. White by William C. White" (see pp. 78, 79).

Do you like horses? Have you ever ridden on a horse? Horses were important to Ellen White. She didn't ride one like a cowboy, but she was often pulled in a buggy or a carriage behind a horse as she traveled around. She and James didn't own a horse or a buggy, but friends often drove them to their meetings.

On one trip, Ellen and James were taken to a friend's house after a meeting. At supper that night, their friends said to Ellen and James, "We have a surprise for you tomorrow." And they wouldn't say what it was.

But that night, while she was sleeping, an angel appeared in Ellen's dream. "Your friends are giving you a buggy tomorrow and money for a horse," the angel said. Why would the angel ruin their surprise? He had a special message for Ellen. He showed her a group of men standing and waiting with three horses.

"They will be there to sell you a horse to pull your buggy." As they watched, a beautiful brown horse pranced around. It was excited and nervous. The angel said, "Don't pick that one." Next they looked at a big gray horse. It was strong but a little clumsy. "Not that one," the angel said. Then they watched the third horse. It was brown with lighter spots. It looked like a smart horse, but its back was bowed in the middle. "This is the one for you," the angel said.

The next morning their friends took them outside. There was a shiny black buggy. "This is our gift to you," they said. They also gave James some money. "Now you can buy a nice horse to pull your buggy as you go to meetings." James was very surprised! But Ellen wasn't.

They walked toward the road where a group of men stood with three horses, just like the angel had shown Ellen. "Please pick one you'd like to pull your buggy as you travel." There they stood: the excited brown horse, the strong gray horse, and the spotted brown horse with the bent back.

Before anyone could say anything, it was Ellen's turn to surprise them. She looked at the dancing brown horse and the big gray horse. Then she pointed to the spotted brown one. "We'll take him," she said.

The spotted brown horse, whose name was Charlie, pulled Ellen and James over many roads to many meetings. Because Ellen listened to the angel's message, she and James had a horse that pulled them safely for years.

Who was Ellen White? She was a person who listened to angels.

Teaching Tips

1. Most children love horses. Ask them to tell any stories they have about horses.

2. What do you think angels would sound like if they spoke to you?

3. Do you think Charlie was the best horse?

Adventist Beliefs for Kids – **25**

CHAPTER 7

Ellen White Saw Visions From God

Questions for Grown-ups

1. Have you ever thought that an illness was an attack by Satan? How would that be different than a regular sickness?

2. What was special about the vision Ellen saw at the funeral?

Do you remember the last time you were sick? Did you have to stay in bed and rest? Did someone take care of you, bringing you food and medicine?

One day Ellen White was sick. She didn't have a sore throat or a fever. She was so sick that she couldn't even move! Ellen and James had traveled on a train to the house of two friends. They were on their way home, but Ellen got so sick that they had to stay with their friends. James and their friends took care of Ellen, but she didn't seem to get better. They were afraid she was going to die.

How did Ellen get so sick? She was attacked!

Not many days before, Ellen and James had been at a funeral. Suddenly, Ellen had a vision. For two hours, she didn't see or hear anything the other people at the funeral did or said. Instead, God was showing her a wonderful story.

Later that day Ellen and James got on the train to start for home. As the train whistle blew and the wheels turned faster and faster, Ellen told James about the vision. She had seen the time before God created the earth,

26 – *Who Was Ellen White?*

when Satan and his angels were thrown out of heaven. She saw the earth created and when Adam and Eve disobeyed God and ate the forbidden fruit. It made her very sad.

But she also heard God's promise to save His children. She saw the days when Jesus came to earth to teach people about God. She saw that when He died on the cross, every person who believed in Him could be saved from sin.

She saw all the way to the end of time, when Jesus will return and Satan will be destroyed. She saw Jesus gather all those who believe in Him and take them home to heaven.

While Ellen was telling James about her vision, someone else was listening. No one on the train could see him, but Satan was there. When he heard what Ellen had seen, he decided, *I cannot allow her to write this story in a book and publish it. I have to stop her.*

Who was Ellen White? She was someone who saw a vision of God's plan to save all of us. What happened to her next? Keep reading these stories, and you will find out.

Teaching Tips

1. Ask the children for stories about when they were sick.

2. What's different about how you feel when you are sick compared to when you are well?

3. In her vision, Ellen saw when God created the earth, the animals and trees, and everything else. What would be your favorite thing to watch if you could see Creation?

4. Why didn't Satan want Ellen to tell what she saw in her vision?

Adventist Beliefs for Kids

CHAPTER 8

Ellen White Wrote Down Visions From God

Questions for Grown-ups

1. As Ellen tried to write down the vision, she got a little stronger each day. What would have happened if she never tried? In what situations should we be willing to try, even when we don't feel like it?

2. Why is *The Great Controversy* such an important book?

To learn more, read *The Great Controversy* (see p. 71).

Earlier we learned that Ellen White was sick—so sick that she might die. But she didn't have a fever or the flu. She could only lie in bed at her friends' house. She couldn't move at all. She was afraid that she would never see her boys again.

When Satan learned that Ellen had seen God's plan to save His people, he decided to stop her before she could write it down in a book. Ellen didn't know it, but he was the one who made her sick. James and her friends didn't know either, but they knew that they should pray. They prayed many times that God would heal her.

Finally, she was strong enough to get on the train and travel home. When they got there, Ellen was so weak that she couldn't play with her children. She could only lie in bed again. But she knew how important her vision was. She wanted to write it down. But for many days, she was too weak to even sit up and write. She prayed that God would heal her, and she kept trying.

Finally, one day she sat up and worked as hard as she could. She wrote one whole page, telling her vision. Then she was too tired to do more. After a few more days, she wrote another page. She kept working until she was writing one page every day. She got stronger and stronger until she could write several pages every day.

It wasn't easy, but Ellen kept working until she had written down everything she saw in the vision. Then James got it printed, and they sent books out to many people. That book became The Great Controversy (con-tro-ver-see), the story of the war between God and Satan.

Later God's angels told Ellen that Satan had attacked her and made her sick after she saw the great-controversy vision. But God had given her the strength to keep writing until the book was done.

Who was Ellen White? She was someone who wrote down the vision God had shown her, even after Satan tried to stop her.

Teaching Tips

1. What did Ellen see in her vision?

2. When did Ellen start getting stronger?

3. What story does the book The Great Controversy tell?

Adventist Beliefs for Kids – **29**

CHAPTER 9

Ellen White Believed in Eating Healthy Food

Questions for Grown-ups

1. Have you seen people who work themselves so hard for God that they get sick? What health or hygiene habits led to them get sick?

2. In Ellen White's day, people knew very little about a healthy lifestyle. If a healthy lifestyle was important to God then, shouldn't it be important to us today?

Do you brush your teeth every day? Do you take a bath? Do you play outside in the sunshine when you can? What about your food—do you eat healthy vegetables and fruits?

Back in the days when Ellen White was alive, people didn't live the same way you do today. Most never brushed their teeth like you do. Many people only took a bath once in the summer and once in the winter. No one had refrigerators back then to keep their food cold and safe from spoiling. Most of the time they couldn't buy vegetables and fruits at the store. If they didn't live on a farm where fruits and vegetables were growing, they didn't have much besides beans and meat to eat.

But they didn't know about healthy living and eating. They didn't know that what you eat and how you live could make you sick. Many of the Adventist preachers and workers got sick. James White had to stop preaching and writing for three years because he was so sick.

By then, Ellen White had seen many visions and had many dreams. She saw heaven and talked with angels. She got messages to pass on to other people about what God wanted them to do. She learned about the war with Satan and God's plan to save His people.

But one day she got a different kind of vision. This time God showed her that He cares about how we live and what we eat. She learned that God wants us to be healthy and happy now like we will be in heaven.

"We must eat healthy food and take care of our bodies," she said. She shared that she had learned that people should stop eating meat and instead eat nuts, fruits, vegetables, and eggs and drink clean milk.

"It is important to stay clean," she told people. "We should wash every day." She also taught them to keep their clothes clean. But she told everyone that the things that were most important for staying healthy or getting well were clean air; sunshine; exercise; and good, clean water.

Who was Ellen White? She was someone who taught that it is important for us to live and eat healthfully if we want to be strong, happy followers of Jesus.

Teaching Tips

1. What do you think would happen if you never brushed your teeth? Or never took a bath? Or never ate any healthy vegetables or fruits?

2. Did you know that God cares about what you eat and drink? Why would that matter to God?

3. Exercise is important to being healthy. What activity do you like to do to get exercise?

Adventist Beliefs for Kids

CHAPTER 10

Ellen White Taught About Health

Questions for Grown-ups

1. What changes in your lifestyle would be needed for you to follow Ellen White's eight principles of health? More sunshine? More rest?

2. How does trusting in God impact your health?

When was the last time you were sick? Did you have a cold, with a runny nose and a fever? Did your stomach hurt? Did you have an earache? Being sick is no fun.

Back when the Adventist Church first got started, people didn't know much about being healthy. Many of the ministers got sick like James White did. Ellen and James's oldest son, Henry, got very sick and died when he was only sixteen years old. Everyone was sad and wondered what to do so they wouldn't get sick so often.

God had an answer. He gave Ellen White a vision about being healthy. And what do you think she did? She started writing books to tell everyone how God wanted them to take care of themselves. People were surprised to learn that God cared about their health.

"There are eight rules about being healthy," she wrote.

1. Fresh air. In Ellen's time, people were afraid that the air might make them sick. They kept their windows closed at night and most of the time during the day. Ellen said, "Open the windows, and let the fresh air in."

2. Sunshine. Back then people didn't know that being out in the sunshine for a few minutes every day is good for us.

3. Not too much of anything. Many of the ministers in those days were working too much. They were eating too much. They needed to learn to be balanced in their lives—just enough work and play and rest.

4. Rest. Sometimes when people are doing things for God or their families, they don't get enough rest. In Ellen's time, they didn't know how important it is to get enough sleep at night.

5. Exercise. People like Ellen and James spent a lot of time riding in buggies or on trains. Did they get enough exercise? Did they walk or run outside every day? Do you?

6. Good food. In Ellen's time, there weren't big grocery stores where you could buy whatever you like to eat. You had to grow your own food or buy it from a farmer. And they didn't have refrigerators to keep their food fresh.

7. Plenty of water. In those days, some people only took a bath once a month or even twice a year! Ellen's vision taught them the importance of drinking plenty of water. They learned that water could help them stay clean and help wash away germs and sickness.

8. Trust in God. Our health is important to God, and trusting Him helps to keep us healthy and happy.

Who was Ellen White? She was someone who knew that God wants us to be healthy.

Teaching Tips

1. When was the last time you were sick? What did you do to get better? Did you go to the doctor? Did your mother or father give you some medicine and make you stay in bed?

2. Do you get enough fresh air and sunshine? Did you play outside today? Ellen White says that these things are important to be healthy.

3. God wants you to be healthy. Will you make the choices to be a healthy person?

Adventist Beliefs for Kids – 33

CHAPTER 10

Ellen White Was the Mother of Four Boys

Questions for Grown-ups

1. What do you do to make Sabbath the happiest day of the week for the children you love?

2. Does it seem as though God should have protected Ellen White's children since she was doing an important work? How do you think she felt when they died?

Ellen and James White had four boys. The oldest was named Henry. A baby boy they named James Edson was born next. (James Edson was called Edson instead.) When Edson was five and Henry was seven, Willie was born. And finally, baby John was born about six years later. For a while, the Whites' home was full of the sounds of children.

Although the boys often stayed with other families when their parents were traveling, their mother spent all the time she could with them when she was at home. They had family worship in the mornings, and then when James went to work, Ellen and the boys would often spend some time working in the flower garden. Then they would play while Ellen wrote her books or letters. They also had worship every evening.

Sabbaths were special in the Whites' home. Ellen did everything she could to make Sabbath the happiest day of the week for her boys. After church, they would often hike nature trails and enjoy the wildlife and the flowers. Sometimes they brought food and had a picnic. When it was cold or rainy and they had to stay in the house, Ellen would read special stories she had found in books and magazines for her boys.

But the boys were not perfect. Often they got in trouble, just like you and I do. They got into things they weren't supposed to. They didn't always get their chores done. And sometimes they got punished. Ellen and James worked hard to make sure that the boys learned to be honest and to obey and, most important, to love God.

But there was sadness in their home too. Baby John only lived for a few weeks. Willie almost drowned in a big tub of water. And when he was only sixteen years old, Henry got sick and died. Ellen White was very, very sad to lose two of her boys. She remembered them every day of her life, but she said, "I will see them again soon in heaven."

As they grew up, Ellen wrote many letters to her boys Edson and Willie. She wrote to them about how much God loved them and how they should follow Him. She always told them how much she loved them. Edson became a worker for God, sharing His good news with many. Willie ended up working with his mother all of her life, living nearby and taking care of her and her writings.

Who was Ellen White? She was the mother of four boys, and she loved each one very much.

Teaching Tips

1. What would it be like if Ellen White was your mother? Would you like to work in the flower garden with her?

2. What does your family do to make Sabbath special?

3. Does it surprise you that Ellen White's boys sometimes got in trouble? Do you ever get in trouble?

Adventist Beliefs for Kids – 35

CHAPTER

Ellen White Was a Woman Who Loved Mountains and Adventure

Questions for Grown-ups

1. Does it surprise you that Ellen White rode horses and liked camping in the mountains?

2. James and Ellen took time away from their important jobs to relax. What should that say to us? Do you ever feel guilty for getting away from work and church responsibilities?

As the Adventist Church began to grow, Ellen White got busier and busier. She and James were often invited to come and preach at churches and camp meetings. Everywhere they went, people wanted to see them and ask them questions. They worked and traveled for so long and got so tired that they needed to rest.

Whenever they had time for a vacation, Ellen and James liked to go to the mountains in Colorado. Ellen loved the fresh air and the beautiful scenery. Sometimes they would go camping high up in the mountains with friends. No, they couldn't jump in their cars and drive to a nice campsite. There weren't any cars or any roads through the mountains then. Instead, they had a real adventure and rode horses, carrying everything they needed to camp.

On one camping trip, Ellen and the others were riding up a trail toward their camping spot. Suddenly, something came loose on Ellen's saddlebag and hit her horse on the leg. Ellen stopped the horse; but before she could get off of it, the horse got scared and jumped. Ellen was thrown into the air and landed hard on the rocky ground. She hit her head and her back and hurt her ankles badly.

She didn't want to miss the camping trip, so she told everyone that she was OK and that they should keep going. Later she found out that her ankles were injured worse than she thought. She had pain and trouble walking for the rest of her life.

Another time Ellen and James joined a large group who were traveling from Texas to Colorado in a wagon train! They traveled each day with strong horses pulling covered wagons just like the pioneers. But they had troubles along the way.

After just three days of traveling, a storm struck while they were still putting up their tent to sleep in. It rained so hard that in just a few moments, the tent floor was covered in several inches of water. All their things were wet, and no one slept well after that.

Along the trail, they had to circle the wagons each night and keep the horses inside. Robbers and outlaws were looking to attack and steal whatever they could. The men took turns staying awake at night to guard their camp. Ellen didn't like this adventure as much as she liked camping in the mountains!

Sometimes Ellen and James took the time for a vacation, but they were always in a hurry to get back to their work of telling people about Jesus.

Who was Ellen White? She was a person who loved the mountains and loved adventure!

Teaching Tips

1. Do you like to take trips or go on vacation? Where do you like to go?

2. Do you think it would have been fun to go with a wagon train with big horses pulling covered wagons? What part would you like most?

3. Do you think God wants us to go on vacations and take trips? Why?

Adventist Beliefs for Kids

CHAPTER 13

Ellen White Was a Woman Who Went Where God Led Her

Questions for Grown-ups

1. Considering how difficult a cross-country train trip was in Ellen White's day, would you have been willing to make that trip so many times?

2. Going anywhere God wants you to go can mean many things. In your life, how have you gone where God wants you to go? Is there somewhere you should be going now?

Have you ever been on a train—a real train that goes racing down the tracks, blowing its whistle at every crossing? In Ellen White's time, the railroads were still being built. Today, if you take a long train ride, you can sit on nice, soft seats and look out the windows. You will be safe and comfortable and stay warm in winter and cool in the summer.

But in Ellen White's day, trains were different. You sat on hard wooden benches with only a metal stove at the front of the car to keep you warm. In summer, it was always hot. Herds of buffalo ran beside the tracks, and cowboys on horses watched over their cattle as the train went by. Those were the days when masked robbers stopped trains and took everyone's money. In winter, the tracks might be covered so deep in snow that the train had to stop. In summer, there might be floods that washed away the tracks.

When Ellen White rode the train from her home in Michigan, it would take almost a week to get to California. But she wanted to see that the people in the West learned about Jesus' soon return. She helped to start churches and schools and hospitals. Even though it might have been cold or dangerous, Ellen White took that train trip more than twenty times!

Have you ever been on a ship? Out on the ocean with big waves? Did you get seasick? I always do. The ship bounces up and down, up and down with the waves. But some people like that—and Ellen was one of those people. When she was on the West Coast, Ellen liked to travel on ships to the meetings and churches.

On one trip, during a storm, everyone else got seasick and went below to rest in their bunks. But not Ellen! She stood on the deck and watched the waves while the ocean spray rained down on her. Later she wrote to James, "The waves ran high and we were tossed up and down so very grandly." She thought it was as much fun as a roller coaster!

Who was Ellen White? She was a person who wasn't afraid to go anywhere that God wanted her to go.

Teaching Tips

1. Have you ever ridden on a train? What did you like most about it?

2. Do you ever get sick on boats? Ellen White didn't. She liked to watch the waves while on big ships in the ocean, and she liked to feel the spray of water on her face.

3. When you grow up, will you go anywhere God wants you to go?

Adventist Beliefs for Kids

CHAPTER 14

Ellen White Was a Woman Who Wanted to Talk About Jesus

Questions for Grown-ups

1. Are missionaries as important today as they were in Ellen White's day? How is the service of a missionary different today?

2. Considering how difficult it is for us to get out of bed and go to church some weeks, what would it take for us to have the will to make a journey such as Ellen's trip to the Pennsylvania camp meeting?

Have you ever wanted to travel to other places in the world? Maybe to Africa to see the lions or the zebras? Or to Australia to see the kangaroos or to China to see the panda bears? Ellen White wanted to go to other places in the world too. But she wanted to go because God had given her more visions.

In one of her visions, she saw how important it was to send missionaries around the world to share the news that Jesus is coming back soon. She began encouraging the church to teach people to speak other languages so that they could share the good news about Jesus everywhere in the world.

Ellen wrote a lot about how important it was to send missionaries to other countries to teach them that Jesus is returning soon. And she showed them how by going herself. Ellen spent years traveling to other countries, teaching and writing and helping to start schools and churches.

But she had to do some trips alone. All through his life, James had worked as hard as Ellen to spread the news about Jesus' soon return. He worked so hard that, in 1881, James got sick and died. Ellen missed him very much, but she kept doing the work God had given her to do. She kept

40 – *Who Was Ellen White?*

going wherever God sent her. Some of those places were in other countries, and some were closer to home.

When Ellen felt that God wanted her to go someplace where she could talk about Jesus, nothing could keep her from going. One summer she was invited to go to a camp meeting in Pennsylvania. But the weather there that spring had brought so much rain that floods had washed away many roads and bridges. "You can't get to the Pennsylvania camp meeting," people said. "Just stay home."

But Ellen didn't listen. She and her friend Sara took the train from her home in Michigan and traveled for several days. Then they were told, "You can't get there on the train. You need to go back home."

But Ellen and Sara went on. When the train couldn't go any farther because the tracks were washed out, they rented a horse and carriage and kept going. When the carriage couldn't go on because the roads and bridges were flooded, they got out and started walking. They walked for many miles until they got to the camp meeting. Then Ellen could talk to the people about God and His love for them.

Who was Ellen White? She was someone who would do anything to go where God wanted her to talk about Jesus.

Teaching Tips

1. Do you think it's important to send missionaries out to tell people about God? Will you be a missionary someday?

2. Does Ellen and Sara's trip sound like fun to you? Which would you like best—the train ride, the carriage ride behind a horse, or walking for four days?

3. Why did Ellen travel to places even when it was hard to do so and took a long time?

Adventist Beliefs for Kids

CHAPTER

Ellen White Wrote Messages for the Whole World

Questions for Grown-ups

1. Have Ellen White's writings been an effective way to spread her messages from God? How do you think she would share her messages if she were alive today?

2. Is it possible to use her writings in a hurtful way? What can we do to avoid doing that to the people around us?

Does it get cold where you live? When it starts to get cold where I live, the leaves on the trees change colors. All summer they are green; but when autumn comes, they turn red or yellow. When the wind blows, the leaves let go of the tree limbs and fly through the air until they fall to the ground. If you live near a lot of trees, there are leaves flying everywhere for a few weeks.

When Ellen White learned something from God in a vision or a dream, she always wanted to write it down. Later she took the things she wrote after her visions and put them into a book. Sometimes she would use them to write an article for a magazine. And many times she wrote letters to people about the things from her visions. She wanted to tell everyone about the things she had learned.

She said, "These things I write about God's plan for us should be spread like the leaves of autumn." That means she wanted the messages to go everywhere. Not just everywhere she went in her buggy or on a train. Not even just everywhere she went in a boat. She wanted the messages to go everywhere in the world!

That's why she and James started taking her books to be printed. Then, to get them out faster, they bought their own printing press to print the books and magazines on. Together they started two publishing houses—first, the Review and Herald® in Michigan, and then the Pacific Press® in California. Both publishing houses printed books and magazines as fast as they could and sent them out in every direction—like the leaves of autumn!

In her lifetime, Ellen wrote forty books and more than five thousand articles for magazines. She also wrote thousands and thousands of letters to people. In her letters, she would often encourage people. But sometimes she told them that God knew when they were doing wrong and that they needed to change and live right. She always told them to read their Bibles and listen to God's voice in their hearts.

Who was Ellen White? She was someone who wanted the messages God gave her to go out to the whole world.

Teaching Tips

1. Do the leaves fall from the trees in autumn where you live? Do you ever rake them into a big pile and jump into them?

2. Why did Ellen want to write so much?

3. Do you think you would like to get a letter from Ellen White?

Adventist Beliefs for Kids – **43**

CHAPTER 16

Ellen White Loved to Tell the Story of Jesus

Questions for Grown-ups

1. Ellen White said that no story is more powerful than the story of Jesus. Have you taken the opportunity to read the story in the Bible and in *The Desire of Ages*?

2. How far would you travel to bring a sick loved one to Jesus for healing? Could anything keep you from finding Him?

Do you have a favorite story? Maybe it's a story about a boy who fights a giant with a sling. Or about a big flood and a lot of animals. Maybe your favorite story is about puppies or kittens or a long trip in a car.

Ellen White had a favorite story too. It was a story she loved to tell over and over. And she turned it into a book, one of her biggest and best-loved books. That book is called *The Desire of Ages*, and it's the story of Jesus.

This is what she said about Jesus when He was a boy: "Jesus didn't grow up in a wealthy home or near a school. He lived in a little mountain village called Nazareth. In the sunlight of His Father's smile, Jesus grew taller, stronger, and wiser. He was a child that people liked and how He acted always pleased God."*

What was Jesus like? She said, "As a child, Jesus was kind to everyone, always patient and honest no matter what. He knew the difference between right and wrong, and He was always unselfish and always polite."

Do you wish you could have played with Jesus when He was your age?

In her book about Jesus, Ellen said that He loved to sing when he was a boy. "When Jesus sang, the people around Him felt better. In fact, everyone was happier when He was around. Older people and children were always happy to see Him coming. Even the little birds in the trees and the donkeys and oxen who were carrying heavy loads seemed happier when He was around."

Ellen also told about how Jesus taught people and healed them. "One day Jesus was at Peter's house. His wife's mother was there also, and she was sick. Jesus healed her, and she felt so good that she got up and helped make dinner. People heard what happened, and that night it seemed like everyone in the city headed toward Peter's house."

What about you? Would you have rushed to Peter's house to see Jesus? What if someone at your house was sick? Would you take the person to Jesus?

That's what everyone did. Ellen White's book says, "For hour after hour, families brought their sick loved ones through the door of Peter's house to be healed by Jesus. They kept coming because no one knew if Jesus would still be there the next morning."

Ellen White's wonderful book about Jesus is something you will want to read someday.

Who was Ellen White? She was someone who loved the story of Jesus.

---

*Quotations in this story are adapted for children from Ellen G. White, *The Desire of Ages* (Nampa, ID: Pacific Press® Pub. Assn., 2005), 68–73, 253–269.

Teaching Tips

1. What's your favorite story?

2. Do you think it would have been fun to play and sing with Jesus when He was your age?

3. When someone in your house is sick, do you wish you could take him or her to Jesus to be healed?

Adventist Beliefs for Kids

CHAPTER 17

Ellen White Believed in Adventist Education

Questions for Grown-ups

1. Is Adventist education important to our church? Why does it matter?

2. What does it mean to learn about God from nature? Have you helped a child learn about God while outdoors?

One day Edson White, Ellen's son, looked out the window of their home in Battle Creek, Michigan, and saw a stranger chopping wood. Strangers often stopped by their house to visit with his mother, but Edson wondered about this one. When he asked, he found out that this man's name was Goodloe Bell. But more important, Mr. Bell was a teacher!

Edson talked to his brother Willie and some friends. "Wouldn't you like to go to a school with a Christian teacher? Let's talk to him." So they went to Mr. Bell. "We'd like you to be our teacher," they said.

Mr. Bell liked the idea of an Adventist school too. He agreed to teach them, and soon they began to meet. Mr. Bell was an excellent teacher, and he expected his students to work hard. When he called a student's name, that student jumped up and stood beside their desk to answer his question.

More families heard about the school, and more kids wanted to attend. Mr. Bell had to find a larger place to meet! He talked with some of the church leaders, and they agreed that the school could use a big, empty room in the Review and Herald® publishing house. It took time to clean

46 – *Who Was Ellen White?*

up the place, and it wasn't pretty. But some long wooden benches were set up for the students, and the school was ready to go.

The first Adventist school was growing, thanks to Mr. Bell and Ellen White's son Edson. The leaders of the church began to see the need for church schools where students could be taught by teachers who loved God and believed in the Bible.*

Today there are thousands of Adventist schools around the world, and they have more than one million students.

Ellen White thought that education was very important. She helped to start many of the schools because she wanted children to learn. She wanted them to learn to read. She wanted them to learn to do math. But most of all, she wanted them to learn about Jesus. She said, "Since God is the source of everything we can learn, the first thing we should do is learn about Him."†

There are two places to learn about God. Ellen said, "The Bible should be the most important schoolbook we have." But we can also learn about God from nature. She said, "As much as possible, children should be able to spend time out in nature. By watching the animals and trees and stars, they can learn about God the Creator."

Who was Ellen White? She was someone who believed in Adventist education.

---

* "Edson's New Teacher," *Ellen White: Visionary for Kids*, Third Quarter 2011.

† Quotations in this story are adapted for children from Ellen G. White, *Education* (Nampa, ID: Pacific Press® Pub. Assn., 2002), 16–19, 99–120.

Teaching Tips

1. Do you have an Adventist teacher in your classroom? What would be better if your teacher was an Adventist?

2. What are the things Ellen White wanted children to learn? What was most important?

3. What have you learned about God by watching animals, trees, and stars?

Adventist Beliefs for Kids

CHAPTER 18

Ellen White Wrote Books About God's Love

Questions for Grown-ups

1. Have you read *Steps to Christ*? What did it teach you about what it means to follow Jesus?

2. *Steps to Christ* teaches us that the story of Jesus tells us what God is like. Based on the book, what is God like?

To learn more, read *Steps to Christ* (see p. 71).

Have you ever followed a path through the woods or across a field, even when you didn't know where it was going? I like to do that. I like to follow along to see what's over the next hill or behind the next tree. I think Ellen White must have liked that too. When she wrote about how to be a Christian, she talked about steps along a path.

One of Ellen White's books that people love most is called *Steps to Christ*. It's all about learning to follow Jesus—learning to be more like Him. In her book, Ellen says the first step is to know that God loves us.

She says, "God loves you. The Bible makes that very clear. But it is also clear from the world around you. Look at the wonders of nature, at how plants and animals live and grow. Look how the sun kisses the earth and rain gives it a drink. This makes the grass and trees cover the ground like a green carpet. And it keeps the rivers and seas full of life."*

Do you see how much God loves you? He created all the things we see in nature to make us happy. And the Bible says that God loves us so much that He sent His Son Jesus to this world to save us.

48 – *Who Was Ellen White?*

In *Steps to Christ*, Ellen White said it this way, "Every flower that blooms and every blade of green grass tells us that 'God is love.' Birds that sing in the sky, flowers that smell so sweet, and the beautiful green leaves of the trees all tell us about God's love. They tell us that He wants to make you and all His children happy."

And that's why Jesus came to our earth. Ellen White's book explains that the story of Jesus tells us what God is like. When we learn that Jesus was always fair and truthful, we know that God cares about doing the right thing. When we learn that Jesus healed sick people and cheered up those who were sad, we know that God cares about how we feel. When we learn that Jesus never hurt another person and was always kind, even to those who hurt Him, we know that God loves every person—including us.

Steps to Christ has shown God's love to millions of people around the world. Ellen White wrote it in English, but it has been translated into Spanish, French, Portuguese, German, and more than 140 other languages!

Who was Ellen White? She was the writer of many books, and they all tell us how much God loves us.

*Quotations in this story are adapted for children from Ellen G. White, *Steps to Christ* (Nampa, ID: Pacific Press® Pub. Assn., 1999), 9, 10.

Teaching Tips

1. Do you have a favorite flower? A favorite bird? A favorite tree?

2. Why did God create all the things we see in nature?

3. What can we learn from knowing that Jesus was kind and never hurt another person?

Adventist Beliefs for Kids

CHAPTER 19

Ellen White Gave Offerings for God's Work

Questions for Grown-ups

1. Have you ever sacrificed to save money for an outreach project?
2. Do you think that God will bless you more if you give money to further the gospel?

Ellen had a secret. She was hiding something behind the cupboard door.

The Whites didn't have much money. James worked wherever he could. Some days he chopped trees to sell for firewood. Some days he plowed fields for a farmer. He did whatever work he could so that his family would have enough money to buy food and clothes and stay warm in their house.

When he was paid for his work, James brought the money home to Ellen. "It's not much," he would say.

Ellen would just smile. "We'll make it last," she told him. But Ellen was working on a special plan. When she bought food, she shopped carefully and spent only a little money. When they needed clothes, she shopped carefully for cloth and sewed the clothes herself.

When she came home with a few extra coins, she went to the cupboard, opened the door, and reached for the stocking that was hanging there on a nail. She dropped the extra coins into the stocking. The clinking sound she heard made her smile.

For months, Ellen had been saving coins whenever she could. One day she noticed that the rugs around the house were getting worn out. They helped to keep the house warm. Should she spend money on new ones? "No," she said to herself. "I'll make rag carpets out of our old clothes."

And so she did. And she was able to add a few more coins to her secret stocking.

Not many days later James came home looking very worried. He had been working at the printing press to get the next magazine ready to send out. "We don't have enough money to buy the paper we need," he said. "We need sixty-four dollars. What can we do?"

Ellen didn't answer. She just went to the cupboard and pulled out her secret stocking. James's mouth fell open when she poured all the coins out onto the table. Together they counted out the money. Would there be enough? Yes! Now James could go and buy the paper they needed to send God's messages out again.

Who was Ellen White? She was someone who gave her own money to send out God's messages.

Teaching Tips

1. Do you have a piggy bank or a special place to save money?

2. What are you saving your money to buy? Or will you give it to God like Ellen and James did?

3. God wants us to support His work with our money. Will you plan to do that when you have a job?

Adventist Beliefs for Kids

CHAPTER 20

Ellen White Was Guided by Angels

Questions for Grown-ups

1. When Ellen White was asked to go to Australia, she wasn't sure it was the right thing to do. But God helped her to understand that she should do what the church asked her to do. How does this apply to us? Should we always do what we are asked to do?

2. Why was it important to build a school first in Australia?

Have you seen kangaroos or koalas in a zoo? Or have you been to Australia? When I visited Australia, I saw kangaroos bouncing across a field, stopping to eat grass like cows. I saw wallabies hopping around. I saw koalas in the trees, chewing on leaves. And the kookaburras were so loud!

In 1891, when she was sixty-four years old, Ellen White was asked by the church to move to Australia and help the Adventists there. So she got on a ship with her family—her son Willie and his children—and the other people who worked for her, and they sailed for weeks across the ocean.

One of the first things Ellen White wanted to do in Australia was help the people there build a school. But first, they needed to buy some land. And they needed a lot of land. They wanted the school to have a farm and an orchard for fruit trees and lots of space. So they began searching for just the right spot.

How would they find a place that wasn't too expensive? How could they be sure that it would have good soil for farming and fruit trees?

Ellen had a dream. In the dream, she saw a piece of land dug up and ready for planting. She saw a man there, looking at the dirt, and he said, "This is not good land for growing things." But she also heard the voice of the angel she often heard in her dreams and visions. The angel said, "It is good soil. It will grow all the vegetables and fruits you need. This is the land you should buy."

Ellen's son Willie was in charge of finding the right land for the school. Ellen traveled with Willie to look at different pieces of land that were for sale. Then they went to a place where she saw a piece of land dug up and ready for planting. While she watched, a man stood over the land and said, "This land is not good for growing things."

But Ellen knew better. "This is the land we want to buy," she told Willie and the others. "This is where our school needs to be."

And they did buy it. Soon a school was being built there. Ellen and Willie and his family built their homes near the new school. And all around them, fruit trees and vegetables grew. It was just the right spot for a school.

Who was Ellen White? She was someone who listened to the angel in her dreams. And because she did so, the Avondale School was built in just the right spot.

Teaching Tips

1. Which animal from Australia do you like best? Kangaroos? Koalas? Kookaburras?

2. In Australia, Ellen White wanted to find some land for a school with enough space for a garden and an orchard. Who helped her find just the right spot?

3. Do you think angels ever talk to you? Do you listen? What do they say?

Adventist Beliefs for Kids – 53

CHAPTER 21

Ellen White Was Kind to Everyone

Questions for Grown-ups

1. Which of Ellen's two ideas for dealing with thieving neighbors would work best for you if you were in that situation?

2. How important is it to show kindness to those around us? How does it affect our ability to share the gospel?

Do you have a dog for a pet? A lot of people like dogs because they are friendly and they are always happy to wag their tails. And people like them because they guard their houses—they bark if anyone comes near the house or if they hear something.

When Ellen White and her family built homes near the new school in Australia, they had a problem. Some of the other people who lived in the same area were not honest. Things began to go missing at Ellen's house. Clothes left out to dry and food prepared and stored for Sabbath simply disappeared. People were stealing these things.

"What can we do?" the others asked Ellen.

Ellen had two ideas. "First," she said, "let's get a dog. He can guard the house and chase burglars away." And that's what they did. They got a dog and named him—wait, what is the name of your dog? Spot? Fred? Max? At Ellen White's house, they named the dog Tiglath-Pileser (tig-lath pill-e-sir). It's a name from the Bible.

Most of the family called the dog Tig. He had a doghouse out behind

Ellen White's house, and he kept a watch on all their things. But he didn't stop all the stealing.

Ellen's second idea took more work. She and Sara got into their buggy and rode out toward the other people's houses. They stopped at a house where a child was sick. "Can we help?" Ellen asked. "Sara is a nurse." So they helped the sick child. Another time they brought good food to people who were hungry.

Before long, Ellen was visiting these neighbors often. When the children gathered around, she would tell stories from the Bible. The children liked her stories—and so did their parents.

As the neighbors got to know Ellen and saw that she was a kind person, the stealing of things at her house stopped. They wanted to know more about her and about the Bible she believed in.

After that, Tig didn't have much guard work to do. He didn't have to stay awake all night. He didn't have to sniff out any burglars or chase any thieves. He was happy to live in his doghouse and be friends with all the people who came to visit Ellen White's house.

Who was Ellen White? She was a person who believed in being kind to everyone.

Teaching Tips

1. Ask the children to share something about a pet, focusing on dogs. Why do people like dogs? What do they do for a family?

2. What did Ellen and Sara do to help their neighbors?

3. What happened when the neighbors learned that Ellen White was a kind person?

Adventist Beliefs for Kids – 55

CHAPTER 22

Ellen White Was Protected by Angels

Questions for Grown-ups

1. It's not uncommon for people to try to disrupt meetings that are telling people about Jesus and about Bible truth. What is the best way to deal with them today?

2. Although she never saw the angel over her tent, Ellen White slept peacefully that night. What can we learn that might help us to sleep peacefully every night?

Have you ever been to a camp meeting? That's when a lot of Adventist families get together for a week or weekend of meetings to learn more about God and about what the Bible teaches. There is always lots of singing and fun.

When Ellen White was in Australia, she went to Australia's first camp meeting. The people had put up a big tent for everyone to gather in. There were also many smaller tents for people to sleep in. Everyone wanted to learn more about Ellen's messages from God. They asked her to be the preacher for many of the meetings.

But some people didn't like that she was the preacher. They didn't like the things she said about Saturday being the Sabbath day. Some didn't like the Adventists at all. They said to each other, "We don't want this meeting going on. And we don't want Ellen White preaching."

Some of those same men came to the meetings, but they didn't come to listen or to learn about Jesus. They came to scare people and to drive them away so they couldn't listen to Ellen White. They threw stones and pulled a tent down. And before they left, they said, "Tomorrow night we're going to tear down Mrs. White's tent—while she's inside it."

Some of the church members heard what they said. "We're afraid that tomorrow night they will come back and hurt you."

But Ellen wasn't afraid. "My angel will guard me and everyone else here for camp meeting." But the people were still worried, so the next day they hired a policeman to watch Ellen's tent and keep her safe.

While Ellen slept peacefully that night, the policeman watched from outside. The dangerous men heard that there was a real policeman guarding her, so they left. But the policeman stayed to keep watch.

Just after midnight he saw a light over Ellen's tent. The light grew brighter and brighter. And inside the light was a silver angel!

Before long, the policeman left and went back to the police station. "What are you doing here?" the other policeman asked. "You're supposed to be guarding that preacher lady."

"She doesn't need me," he answered. "She has an angel guarding her tent. But I'm going back there tomorrow night. I want to hear what she's saying."

And he did go back. The more he listened, the more he believed. Before long, he decided to follow God and become an Adventist too.

Who was Ellen White? She was someone who was protected by an angel.

Teaching Tips

1. Have you ever been to a camp meeting? What did you like best about it, or what do you think would be the most fun if you haven't gone to one?

2. The people who tried to scare everyone were bullies. How do you deal with bullies at your school?

3. Do you believe that angels watch over you at night when you sleep, like Ellen's angel watched over her?

Adventist Beliefs for Kids – **57**

CHAPTER 23

Ellen White Received Messages for Her Family

Questions for Grown-ups

1. What would it be like to be a part of Ellen White's household, knowing that she might have a message for you on any day? Would that make you happy or nervous?

2. Have you ever received an answer to prayer that wasn't the one you wanted? Did you accept it or pray for a different answer?

For more stories, read *Glimpses Into the Life of Ellen White* (see p. 71).

What would it be like if your grandmother talked to angels? What if she got messages from God? What if she got messages about you?

When Ellen White moved to Australia, her son Willie and his children moved, too, and built a house near hers at Avondale, where the new school was being built. Since there were no hotels there, the only places for visitors to stay were in people's homes. Many stayed at Ellen White's house. But if her house was full, then the people came to stay at Willie's house.

Ellen's oldest granddaughter, Ella, wasn't always happy to see guests. They meant a lot of extra work—extra cooking, extra cleaning, and extra laundry. But the job Ella hated most was cleaning the big kettles. In those days, cooking for a lot of people meant using a big kettle—a heavy iron bucket—that sat right on the hot wood-burning stove.

One of Ella's chores was to clean the big kettles. But she couldn't just rinse them out and put them in the dishwasher. There were no dishwashers in those days. No, she had to drag them out of the house to a big sandpit. There she used the sand to scrub the kettles until they were clean again.

58 – *Who Was Ellen White?*

But she didn't like it. She started to pray that God would give a message to her grandmother to tell her parents not to make her clean the kettles. Not many days later Ellen stopped by Willie's house for a visit, as she often did. But this time she had a message for the family.

From a paper in her purse, Ella's grandmother first read a message from God for Willie. Then she read a message for Willie's wife. Ella hoped she was finished. But no, next she read a message for Ella! "Ella, you should help your mother more."

When Ella heard that, it made her mad! She wanted a message that said she should do fewer chores, not more! So she asked her grandmother, "Did the angel really tell you that? Or did you just make it up?"

Her grandmother looked at her and said, "I didn't write anything except what the angel told me."

When she left, Ella ran to her room, threw herself on her bed, and cried. "It's not fair," she said to herself. "I prayed for less work to do, and the angel said I should do more." But suddenly, she thought, *It is an answer to my prayer. Just not the answer I wanted.*

Ella never forgot that the God of heaven had taken time to send an angel with a message just for her.

Who was Ellen White? She was someone who got a message from an angel—just for her granddaughter!

Teaching Tips

1. What if your grandmother talked to angels? What if they had a message for you?

2. Have you ever had chores you didn't like to do? Did you do them anyway?

3. Ella got a message about doing chores but not the one she wanted. What did she do? What would you do?

Adventist Beliefs for Kids

CHAPTER 24

Ellen White Trusted God to Keep His Promises

Questions for Grown-ups

1. What would God have to say to you before you were willing to move your whole family halfway across the world? Could you ever be sure He was the one speaking to you?

2. God kept His promise and led Ellen to the house she needed. Can you think of a time when God kept a promise to you?

Ellen White and her workers and her son Willie and his family were settled in Australia. The new school and health center were open. The Adventist Church was growing. But then one morning, Ellen surprised everyone. "We must move back to the United States," she said. "God is telling me that we must go back."

"Are you sure?" Willie asked. "I know you love living here."

Ellen did want to stay in Australia, but she nodded. "We must go where God tells us."

So the family began to pack up their things and get ready for the long trip to America. They sold their houses and said good-bye to their friends. Soon they were boarding a big steamship. It would take twenty-three days to cross the ocean and get to California.

Ellen enjoyed sailing, but she spent many hours praying about where they would live. Could they find a house that had enough room for her and all her helpers? Could they find a quiet place where she could write her books and letters? One evening God spoke to Ellen and promised that He had a special place ready for her to live. She didn't need to worry about it anymore.

When the ship landed in San Francisco, Ellen and Willie began looking for a place to live. Ellen wanted to live in California because it was warm there, and she could be near Pacific Press®, where her books would be printed. But no house they looked at seemed right. Finally, Willie said, "Mother, why don't you go up to the health center at St. Helena and get some rest?"

Ellen did. She took Sara, her friend and nurse, and some other people and went eighty miles north of the city to the health center. While she was there, she heard about a house that was for sale nearby. She took the horse and buggy out to see it.

It was a large white house with elm trees in the front yard. There were flowers around the house—mostly roses, which Ellen loved to see and smell. Behind the house were orchards full of peaches and apples and pears and cherries and a garden full of vegetables. The house and the buildings around it would be big enough for Ellen and her workers and all her papers. There wasn't room for Willie and his family, but there was a nice spot to build a house for them not far away.

Ellen had found the special place God had promised her. Because of the elm trees in the yard, they called it Elmshaven. It was Ellen's home for the rest of her life.

Who was Ellen White? She was someone who trusted God to keep His promises.

Teaching Tips

1. Why did Ellen White say that her family should move back to the United States from Australia?

2. Have you ever been on a big ship in the ocean? Were you worried about the waves? Did you see any whales?

3. Do you ever worry about things that might happen? Do you pray, like Ellen did, and listen to God's voice in your heart?

Adventist Beliefs for Kids

CHAPTER 25

Ellen White Loved Her Grandchildren

Questions for Grown-ups

1. Was Sara doing the right thing in keeping people away from Ellen White?

2. Ellen White loved her grandchildren. How would you balance your love of your children or grandchildren with a task you believe God has given you to do?

As Ellen White got older, she spent more time at home, writing her books and letters. She had helpers who made copies of the things she wrote. She had a man who took care of the orchards and farm. She had a cook who made the meals for everyone. But her most important helper was Sara. Sara was her friend and her nurse. She made sure that Ellen was taken care of all the time.

Sara also made sure that no one bothered Ellen when she was writing or resting. Not visitors who came to the house, not important church people—not even Ellen's grandchildren. Willie and his family had built a house nearby, and the grandchildren often came to Elmshaven to play. But Sara would say, "Run along, children. You know your grandmother is busy today. She doesn't have time for you."

But Ellen was the kind of grandmother who liked to see her grandchildren. And her grandchildren always wanted to see her. But to see their grandmother, they had to get past Sara.

So they would wait until Sara was in the front part of the house, maybe at the front door telling visitors that they couldn't see Ellen now. But the children knew something that visitors didn't know: there was a back door at Elmshaven that led to a back stairway. And at the top of those stairs was their grandmother's writing room.

Shhh! they would whisper to each other. They opened the back door very slowly and quietly. Then up the little stairway they went, just as slowly and quietly. They knew that one wooden step squeaked every time someone stepped on one side of it. They didn't want Sara to hear them, so they each stepped carefully. The children knew that Grandma Ellen was busy and that her work was important. They didn't understand everything she did or all the things she wrote. But they knew that it was important, and they didn't want to bother her. All they wanted was to see her for a few minutes.

So they had an agreement with her. When they came up the stairs and into her writing room, they would wait quietly until she laid her writing pen down. That was the signal. Now they could run across the room and climb up on her lap. She would give each one a hug and kiss. She would tell them how much she loved them—and how much God loved them. Before long, she would send them out to play somewhere else.

They would go back down the stairs slowly and quietly. They stepped carefully around the squeaky step. Then out the back door they would go, heading off for fun somewhere else.

And Sara never knew they were there.

Who was Ellen White? She was a grandmother who loved her grandchildren.

Teaching Tips

1. Do you like to visit with your grandmother? Do you have to sneak into her house to see her?

2. How did Ellen's grandchildren sneak in to see her?

3. Even though they wanted to see her, Ellen's grandchildren didn't want to disturb her important work. What signal did they wait for before they ran across the room?

Adventist Beliefs for Kids –

CHAPTER 26

Ellen White Liked to Have Fun With Her Family

Questions for Grown-ups

1. Are you surprised to learn that Ellen White liked to have fun? That she liked riding in a buggy, riding in a car with her grandsons, or watching the family play baseball?

2. What can you do to make Sabbath special for your family, especially the children? What are you doing?

Ellen spent a lot of time writing more books and letters. Her workers kept busy helping her make copies of the things she wrote. But it wasn't all work at Elmshaven. Ellen liked to have fun with her family.

Almost every day Ellen and Sara took a buggy ride on the roads near Elmshaven. Many times one grandchild or another would go along in the buggy. The horse would pull them down the road, and they would enjoy the fresh air. Sometimes they would stop to visit with a neighbor or check on some of the farm animals. Every ride with Grandma Ellen was fun.

But one day it was the grandchildren's turn to take Grandma Ellen for a ride. In those days, cars had only been around for a few years and very few people had one. Most everyone was still being pulled around by horses, just like Ellen. But when her two grandsons were old enough, they bought a car. And one of the first things they wanted to do was to take Grandma Ellen for a ride. This was one of the first times that Ellen rode in a car. And she thought it was great fun!

Sometimes, on a special day, the family would gather behind the house and play baseball. Grandma Ellen would stay on the porch and cheer as the kids hit the ball and ran around the bases.

But there was one very special day every week—Sabbath! Do you like picnics? That's what Ellen's grandchildren liked best on Sabbaths. Many times, after Grandma Ellen was finished preaching and church was over, the family would stop on the way home and have a picnic.

Usually, the kids would go on a nature hike first, but soon the food was ready, and they all ate together on the grass. After lunch, Grandma Ellen might share a letter sent to her by a missionary in a faraway country. Sometimes someone would read from Grandma Ellen's newest book. But no one was in a hurry to go; no one was too busy to spend time together.

The children always liked to eat at Grandma Ellen's house too. Besides having lots of good food, you only had to eat the food you liked. Her rule was, "If you don't want any, then pass it on." When the big bowl of potatoes was passed to you, you put some on your plate if you wanted. If the bowl was full of corn or carrots or something you didn't like, you didn't need to wrinkle up your nose or say, "Yuck!" You just passed the bowl on to the person beside you.

Who was Ellen White? She was someone who liked to have fun with her family.

Teaching Tips

1. Would you like to ride in a buggy behind a horse with Grandma Ellen? Would you be brave enough to ride in a car if you had never seen one before?

2. Does your family do something special on Sabbath—a nature hike, a picnic, or a special story?

3. Do you wish you could have eaten at Grandma Ellen's house, where you only had to eat what you liked and pass it on if you didn't?

Adventist Beliefs for Kids – 65

CHAPTER 27

Ellen White Loved Family Worship

Questions for Grown-ups

1. Family worship happens in many ways in different families. What can we learn from the worships at Elmshaven every Friday night?

2. Do the children in your life get a chance to pray out loud in front of people? Ellen White thought that it was important that every child be comfortable saying a short prayer.

Do you have family worship at your house? It's fun to gather together and read Bible stories or sing! Ellen liked to have everyone come to her house for worship on Friday night. Willie and his wife and the grandchildren would come down the hill from their house. The other helpers and workers who lived nearby with their families would come also. Any visitors who were there that day were invited to stay and join the family.

What do you think family worship was like at Ellen White's house? Well, when everyone was gathering, Ellen would come down from her writing room. She would sit in her chair by the fire and ask for someone to pick a song they could all sing. There wasn't a piano at Elmshaven, but there was a small organ, and someone would play the hymns. Ellen loved to sing at family worship!

When they were finished singing, Ellen would read a few verses from the Bible. She knew that children had a hard time sitting still, so she always kept the family worship short. Then, when she was finished reading, it was time for prayer.

At Ellen White's family worship, everyone prayed. It didn't matter who was there—the president of the world church, a farmer, or just the family. She wanted everyone to have a chance to pray out loud, especially the children. They were short prayers—just a sentence or two. But the children always got to pray just like the adults.

When Ellen was a child, she was too shy to pray out loud. She didn't want any of her grandchildren or great-grandchildren to be afraid to pray in front of others. So she made sure they got to do it every week!

Did you know that you can travel to Elmshaven and see the house where Ellen White lived? Today Elmshaven is kept like a museum. If you visit, you can come in and sit in the same room that Ellen White's grandchildren did when they came to her house for family worship. Her chair is still there by the fireplace. You can imagine singing and praying just like you were part of her family.

Who was Ellen White? She was someone who loved family worship.

Teaching Tips

1. Do you have family worship in your house? If you do, what's your favorite thing about family worship? The singing? The stories?

2. What's your favorite song to sing at worship or at Sabbath School?

3. Do you get to pray out loud in front of others? Are you afraid to?

Adventist Beliefs for Kids

CHAPTER 28

Ellen White Was God's Messenger

Questions for Grown-ups

1. Ellen White wrote and traveled and preached around the world because God asked her to. What is God asking you to do?

2. At the time, it discouraged a lot of people when Ellen White died because they thought God would keep her alive until the Second Coming. What does it say to you to know that Ellen White died like any other person?

As the years went by, Ellen got older and weaker. She couldn't travel across the country on a train anymore. She couldn't take a sailboat out onto the ocean. She couldn't preach as often or read as much as she wanted to. But there was one thing she could still do. She could write her books!

Ellen and her helpers worked hard to finish the books she had planned. She could only work on the writing for a few hours each day before she needed to rest. But she kept writing. She wanted to finish the work God had given her.

Although Sara or another nurse was always nearby, one day Ellen tripped and fell before anyone could catch her. She was hurt badly—her hip was broken. The doctor and nurses did all they could, but they couldn't make her better. A few months later, on July 16, 1915, Ellen White died. She was eighty-seven years old.

Why did God let her die? Because her work was finished. Ellen had done what God asked her to do so many years before. She had taken His messages to the world.

During her life, God sent Ellen more than two thousand visions and dreams. Sometimes she saw angels or heard them sing. Some visions were about healthy living, some were about education, and some were about people. But whatever the message was, Ellen passed it on. She preached to many thousands of people. She traveled all over the world on ships and trains. Everywhere she went, she talked about God's love and His plans for His people.

Ellen wrote fifty thousand pages of books and articles and many thousands of letters. And she didn't have a computer—she wrote every word on every page with a pen or a pencil.

Why did she travel and preach so often? Why did she write so many words on pages? Because that is what God asked her to do.

What do you think God will ask you to do when you grow up? Will you be a preacher or a doctor or a farmer or a firefighter? Will you be a teacher or a builder or a scientist? Or will you be a writer like Ellen? Whatever God asks you to do, you can make a difference to the people around you by being kind and honest. Whatever God asks you to do, you can help take His message of love to the world.

Who was Ellen White? She was God's messenger.

Teaching Tips

1. When Ellen White was old, she couldn't travel anymore. But there is one thing she could do, do you remember what it was?

2. Why did God let Ellen White die?

3. What do you think God will ask you to do when you grow up?

Adventist Beliefs for Kids – **69**

References

"Edson's New Teacher." *Ellen White: Visionary for Kids*. Third Quarter 2011.

Levterov, Theodore N. *Accepting Ellen White*. Nampa, ID: Pacific Press® Pub. Assn., 2017.

Miller, Mabel R. *Ellen, the Girl With Two Angels*. Nampa, ID: Pacific Press® Pub. Assn., 1998.

Nix, James R. *Glimpses Into the Life of Ellen White*. Nampa, ID: Pacific Press® Pub. Assn., 2016.

White, Ellen G. *Christian Experience and Teachings of Ellen G. White*. Nampa, ID: Pacific Press® Pub. Assn., 1999.

———. *The Desire of Ages*. Nampa, ID: Pacific Press® Pub. Assn., 2005.

———. *Education*. Nampa, ID: Pacific Press® Pub. Assn., 2002.

———. *The Great Controversy*. Nampa, ID: Pacific Press® Pub. Assn., 2005.

———. *Steps to Christ*. Nampa, ID: Pacific Press® Pub. Assn., 1999.

White, William C. "Sketches and Memories of James and Ellen G. White." *Advent Review and Sabbath Herald*. April 25, 1935.

The Williamsport Camp Meeting
Ellen White: Woman of Vision, pp. 258, 259

Thursday night, May 30, Ellen White, accompanied by Sara McEnterfer, boarded the train in Battle Creek bound for Williamsport, Pennsylvania, where the camp meeting was to open Tuesday, June 4. Because of heavy rains, the train moved slowly. They had expected to reach Williamsport the next afternoon at 5:00, but soon they could see that this objective could not be met. Bridges had been swept away and roads washed out by the Johnstown Flood. When they reached Elmira, New York, they were advised to give up their journey.

But neither Ellen nor Sara was easily dissuaded. They were determined to go as far as possible, hoping that the reports concerning the conditions of travel were exaggerated. At Canton, some 40 miles (64 kilometers) from Williamsport, their car was switched onto a side track because of a washout; they spent the Sabbath there in a hotel. Determined to get through, Ellen and Sara put their heads together and left no stone unturned in their attempts to find a way. Traveling by carriage part of the way and walking part of the way, they compassed the 40 miles (64 kilometers) in four days, in a hair-raising venture described in her report in the *Review and Herald* of July 30, 1889. One interesting feature was the manner in which she was sustained physically. She reported:

> We were obliged to walk miles on this journey, and it seemed marvelous that I could endure to travel as I did. Both of my ankles were broken years ago, and ever since they have been weak. Before leaving Battle Creek for Kansas, I sprained one of my ankles and was confined to crutches for some time; but in this emergency I felt no weakness or inconvenience, and traveled safely over the rough, sliding rocks.

At one point they waited for three hours as, at their direction, a raft was constructed upon which to ferry the carriage in which they traveled across a swiftly flowing stream. A small boat pulled it across, the horses swam the stream, and the two women travelers were rowed across. Then they continued their journey by horse and carriage. The destruction reminded Ellen White of what is to come in the last days and encouraged her to be even more diligent in preparation for that day. Her report in the *Review* closes with these words:

> We arrived at Williamsport at three o'clock Wednesday afternoon. The experience and anxiety through which I passed on this journey greatly exhausted me in mind and body; but we were grateful that we had suffered no serious trouble, and that the Lord had preserved us from the perils of the land, and prospered us on our way.

When they reached the town they were told that the campground had been flooded out and that the tents had been taken down. Actually, they found the tents had been moved to higher ground and the meeting was in progress.

Brighton Camp Meeting, Victoria, Australia

Reported by Fairly Masters, member in Australia, reported in a letter written to F. D. Nichol, dated March 20, 1950.

While the first Australian Seventh-day Adventist Bible School was being held in Georges Terrace, St. Kilda, Melbourne, Sister White was with us and during that time the first Australian camp meeting was held at Brighton Beach. We all, students and teachers and Sister White and her staff of workers attended and were camped on the camp ground. I was chosen to man a few young men students to police the mission compound.

Sister White conducted the main preaching services during the first two days and her topic was The Commandments of God—especially the Sabbath—and the truths [regarding] the coming of Christ in the closing scenes of this earth's history in sin.

Well, this stirred Satan, the enemy of Christ. Soon the larrikins mustered in opposition and they first threw stones and pulled down a tent, and my fellow police students reported to me that those hoodlums had threatened then that the next night they would storm and vent their hatred on Mrs. White and her tent.

I reported this to the school faculty and they decided to procure police assistance from Melbourne headquarters to protect Sister White and they sent along a sturdy Irish policeman—a Roman Catholic.

On his arrival the next night I stationed him by Sister White's tent, letting him know who she was, and the intentions of the larrikins, and I told my student young men police to station on the outside of the grounds close to the dwelling tents and let the larrikins know that we had a city policeman guarding Sister White's tent.

Well, as the night began, on came the enemy and they were told that we had a city policeman guarding Mrs.

White's tent. The news quieted them some and later they retired, but the constable kept his close watch on Sister White's tent and she had been told of the procedure. But she did not get alarmed and said her guardian angel from heaven would also protect her and all on the camp ground and she slept in perfect peace.

Soon after midnight the policeman noticed a light forming on Sister White's tent and in that light a silver colored angel appeared.

The constable retired later and reported himself at the city police watch house.

They demanded an explanation which was accepted, and that constable attended the rest of the main preaching services of the camp meeting, accepted this Advent faith and became one of our most ardent church members and finally settled in a town out in the country.

Yes, friends, truly does the Bible tell us of man's heavenly angel guard, and the promise of God's care for His people in this earth comes to our mind afresh in the light of the above instance, and the words are found in Psalm 91:9-11:

"Because thou hast made the Lord,
which is my refuge,

even the most High thy habitation,

there shall no evil befall thee,

neither shall any plague come nigh thy dwelling.

For he shall give his angels charge over thee

to keep thee in all thy ways."

May God give us grace to comply with the conditions upon which the angel guard is promised and all will be well.

Signed, Fairly Masters

The Health Reform Vision

James and Ellen White visited Otsego, Michigan, over the weekend, to encourage the evangelistic workers there. As the group bowed in prayer at the beginning of the Sabbath, Ellen White was given a vision of the relation of physical health to spirituality, of the importance of following right principles in diet and in the care of the body, and of the benefits of nature's remedies—clean air, sunshine, exercise, and pure water.

Previous to this vision, little thought or time had been given to health matters, and several of the overtaxed ministers had been forced to become inactive because of sickness. This revelation on June 6, 1863, impressed upon the leaders in the newly organized church the importance of health reform. In the months that followed, as the health message was seen to be a part of the message of Seventh-day Adventists, a health educational program was inaugurated. An introductory step in this effort was the publishing of six pamphlets of 64 pages each, entitled, *Health, or How to Live*, compiled by James and Ellen White. An article from Mrs. White was included in each of the pamphlets. The importance of health reform was greatly impressed upon the early leaders of the church through the untimely death of Henry White at the age of 16, the severe illness of Elder James White, which forced him to cease work for three years, and through the sufferings of several other ministers. Early in 1866, responding to the instruction given to Ellen White on Christmas Day, 1865 (*Testimonies for the Church*, vol. 1, p. 489), that Seventh-day Adventists should establish a health institute for the care of the sick and the imparting of health instruction, plans were laid for the Western Health Reform Institute, which opened in September 1866. While the Whites were in and out of Battle Creek from 1865 to 1868, Elder White's poor physical condition led them to move to a small farm near Greenville, Michigan. Away from the pressing duties of church headquarters, Ellen White had opportunity to write, and she undertook the presentation of the conflict story as it had been shown to her more fully in further revelations. In 1870, *The Spirit of Prophecy*, volume 1, was published, carrying the story from the fall of Lucifer in heaven to Solomon's time. Work with this series was broken off, and it was seven years before the next volume was issued.

This chapter is taken from Arthur L. White, *Ellen White: A Brief Biography* (Silver Spring, MD: Ellen G. White Estate, 2000).

Gift of a Horse and Carriage
The Advent Review and Sabbath Herald, April 25, 1935
"Sketches and Memories of James and Ellen G. White" by William C. White

Often the methods of travel were wearisome and painful. In order to meet one appointment at Sutton, Vermont, it was necessary to travel forty miles by stage, over the hilly, rough, and dusty roads. As fresh relays of horses were provided every ten miles, Mrs. White availed herself of the privilege of resting for ten minutes at a hotel, for she was very weak.

Some of the brethren who attended this meeting at Sutton, were warm-hearted and generous, and anxious to see the message go. They decided that Elder and Mrs. White should have a conveyance of their own. So they made up a purse of $175 with which to purchase a horse and carriage. Then it was arranged for some of the brethren who had horses for sale to bring them to a certain place on a Monday morning, that Elder and Mrs. White might make their selection.

During the night preceding the day when the horse was to be selected, Ellen White was given a vision in which she saw a company of about twenty men assembled at the crossroads, and three horses brought forward for inspection. The first was a high-spirited sorrel, rather nervous. As they were observing his movements, the angel that was acting as her guide, said to her, "Not that one." Next there was brought forward a large gray horse, clumsy footed and rather awkward. Again her guide said, "Not that one." The third was a large, beautiful dapple chestnut. He had an intelligent face, an arched neck, and was swaybacked. As this horse was led forward, her guide said, "That is the one for you."

The fulfillment of the vision was complete and exact. When they arrived at the place designated for the selection of a horse, they met the very company that had been shown to Ellen White in vision the preceding night. Three horses were brought forward for inspection, exactly as presented to her—the nervous sorrel, the clumsy gray, and then old Charlie, the big dapple chestnut. The selection was quickly made, and horse, harness, and covered buggy were given to Elder White.

Of their first journey to Canada East, known today as Quebec, with their own horse and carriage, Ellen White wrote:

"My throat troubled me much, and I could not speak aloud, or even whisper, without suffering. We rode, praying as we went for strength to endure the journey. About every ten miles we were obliged to stop that I might rest. My husband braided the tall grass and tied the horse to it, giving him a chance to feed, then spread my cloak upon the grass for a resting place for me. Thus we continued until we arrived at Melbourne."—*Id., p. 270*.

The trips made with horse and buggy were among the most enjoyable and restful experiences in the life of these careworn and overworked ambassadors. Their first horse was a source of many pleasant memories. Old Charlie was very fond of apples. Sometimes, when they were driving in the autumn where orchards lined the roads, and big ripe apples lay in the path of the travelers, Elder White loosened the check-rein, and left the horse free to show what he would do. And Charlie appreciated his privileges. When approaching an apple tree with apples on the ground, he would gently slow down from a seven-mile pace, select a good apple within easy reach, pick it up, and then throw his head high and dash on at full speed, eating the apple as he journeyed. Old Charlie never knew how much his master suffered later on from criticism because he drove so good a horse.

Adventist Beliefs for Kids – **79**